Nirvana

Hawks

NorthWord Press

Chanhassen, Minnesota

To my wife, Aubrey, the love of my life
and to my good buddy, Dr. Gordon Court, the raptor junkie. –W. L.

© NorthWord Press, 2004

Photography © 2004:
Richard Day/Daybreak Imagery: cover, pp. 15, 16, 18; Michael H. Francis: pp. 4, 44; Donald M. Jones: pp. 5, 11, 26-27, 29, 35, 40; Jeff Vanuga: p. 8; Gary Kramer/garykramer.net: p. 21; C. Allan Morgan: pp. 24-25; Wayne Lynch: back cover, pp. 10, 13, 14, 20, 28, 30, 33, 34, 36, 38-39, 41, 42-43.

Illustrations by Fred Smith
Designed by Russell S. Kuepper
Edited by Kristen McCurry
Front cover image: Red-tailed hawk (*Buteo jamaicensis*)

NorthWord Press
18705 Lake Drive East
Chanhassen, MN 55317
1-800-328-3895
www.northwordpress.com

Library of Congress Cataloging-in-Publication Data

Lynch, Wayne.
  Hawks / Wayne Lynch ; illustrations by Fred Smith.
     p. cm. – (Our wild world series)
  Includes index.
  Summary: Discusses the physical characteristics, behavior, habitat, and life cycle of hawks.
  ISBN 1-55971-885-4 (hc) – ISBN 1-55971-886-2 (sc)
  1. Hawks—Juvenile literature. [1. Hawks.] I. Smith, Fred, 1951 Dec. 30- ill. II. Title. III. Series.

QL696.F32L96 2004
598.9'44—dc22

                                        2003059998

Printed in Malaysia

10 9 8 7 6 5 4 3 2 1

Our **WILD**™
WORLD
SERIES

Hawks

Wayne Lynch
Illustrations by Fred Smith

NORTHWORD PRESS
Chanhassen, Minnesota

HAWKS LIVE IN surprising ways. In the burning heat of the Arizona desert, Harris's hawks hunt like wolves in packs of four and five. In the cold Arctic, rough-legged hawks tear scraps of frozen meat from the bodies of seals killed by polar bears. In the dark spruce forests of Alaska and Canada, the northern goshawk (GOSS-hawk) attacks hares with the fierceness of a warrior. And in the prairies every autumn, the powerful Swainson's hawk leaves the big skies and soars south for two months to reach the center of South America, a distance of 6,000 miles (9,654 km). There, the Swainson's hawks spend the winter eating grasshoppers, with anteaters and armadillos as their neighbors. Then in the spring, the hawks circle and soar their way back to North America, where they live all summer with badgers and white-tailed deer. Here, the hawks hunt ground squirrels, ground squirrels, and more ground squirrels.

In autumn, most red-tailed hawks leave Alaska and Canada and migrate to the central and southern United States for the winter.

The largest feathers on a redtail are at the tip of the bird's wings. Biologists call these large feathers primaries.

Hawks are called birds of prey (PRAY), or raptors (RAP-torz). They hunt and eat other animals, or prey, for their living. A hawk's most important features are its head, feet, and wings.

To begin with, a hawk's eyes are very big. The coffee-colored eyes of a red-tailed hawk are almost as large as those of an adult human, even though the human is 50 times heavier than the hawk. A hawk's large eyes are very sensitive to details, so these birds see much better than a human does. For example, if a hawk and a human stood at one end of a football field, the hawk could easily see a grasshopper hop across the goal line at the other end of the field. The poor-sighted human would have to walk more than half the length of the field before he could hope to see the grasshopper leap for the touchdown.

Hawks
FUNFACT:

Hawks live all over North America, from the High Arctic tundra of Canada to the prairies, mountains, forests, and deserts of the United States. One of the best places to watch hawks is on the prairies, where there are no trees to hide them from view.

The following popular hawk-watching areas are indicated by the numbers above. The arrows show the hawks' autumn migration routes.

1. Hawk Mountain, Pennsylvania
2. Cape May, New Jersey
3. Holiday Beach, Ontario
4. Hawk Ridge, Minnesota
5. Coastal Bend, Texas
6. Manzano Mountains, New Mexico
7. Goshute Mountains, Nevada
8. Golden Gate, California
9. Cardel, Veracruz, Mexico

The ferruginous hawk, like all hawks, has a bony ridge above its eyes, which gives the bird a fierce appearance.

In many hawks, the color of their eyes changes as they get older. When woodland hawks such as the northern goshawk, Cooper's hawk, and sharp-shinned hawk hatch they have gray eyes. At one year old, their eyes are yellow or orange. A year or two after that, they change to darker shades of red. Eye color does not affect how well a hawk sees, but it does tell its companions how old it is. In this way, a female hawk searching for an older, more experienced male partner only needs to check the color of his eyes to see if he would make a good father for her chicks.

Hawks have a third eyelid, called the nictitating (NICK-ti-tay-ting) membrane, that protects their large, sensitive eyes. This glassy-looking membrane sweeps over the eye from the inside corner and protects it in dangerous situations where the eye might be accidentally injured. This might happen when hawks fight with each other, when they feed their chicks beak-to-beak, or when they fly through shrubs or branches to chase a rabbit or bird.

Hawks
FUNFACT:

The smallest hawk in North America is the sharp-shinned hawk. It's about the size of a blue jay. The largest is the ferruginous hawk of the prairies. The ferruginous hawk is more than 10 times heavier than the sharp-shinned, and has a wingspan of 56 inches (142 cm), nearly the height of an average adult man.

The small beak on a rough-legged hawk matches the small size of its common prey, the lemming. Hawks with larger beaks are able to cut and tear apart the tough skin of larger prey.

Most hawks use their excellent vision to find and catch their prey. It is different for most owls, which hunt at night and rely on their sharp hearing to help them. One hawk, the northern harrier (HAIR-ee-er), is a daytime hawk that often hunts like a nighttime owl. The harrier has a round face, just like an owl. The harrier also has sensitive ears, which it uses to locate mice and similar rodents called voles hidden under shrubs and grass. When it is windy, the harrier can no longer hear the faint rustles of rodents running under the grass. Then it must use its eyes to hunt like other hawks.

Hawks
FUNFACT:

Most male and female hawks have similar coloring. The northern harrier is different. The male is gray and white, and the female is brown.

The long legs of the northern harrier help the bird to reach voles and mice hidden in thick grass.

Hawks have beaks like butcher knives that they use to slice their meals into bite-sized pieces. A hawk's beak grows all its life and always stays sharp from regular use. In zoos, hawks are sometimes fed foods that are too soft for them, so their beaks do not wear down as much as they do in the wild. If the beak grows too much, the hawk cannot eat properly. When this happens, a zookeeper must file off the extra growth on the bird's beak before it can eat normally again.

The fearsome feet of a hawk are its best weapon in making a kill. Three toes face forward and a fourth toe faces backward. Each toe on a hawk's foot ends with a long, sharp claw, called a talon (TAL-un). The fourth toe usually has the longest talon. When a hawk grabs an unlucky victim, it is often this long talon that kills the prey. Hawks have a powerful grip, and they squeeze their prey over and over again until it dies. Hawks with the largest feet and strongest talons hunt the biggest prey, such as rabbits and ground squirrels. Bird-hunting hawks, such as the sharp-shinned hawk and Cooper's hawk, are smaller, but they have especially long toes and talons. This helps them to penetrate, or pierce through, the fluffy feathers that cover their prey.

Hawks
FUNFACT:

Female hawks are larger and stronger than the males. The size difference is greatest in the accipiters. For example, the female sharp-shinned hawk weighs almost twice as much as the male.

After a summer thunderstorm, a juvenile Swainson's hawk spreads its wings to dry its feathers in the sunshine.

The broad tail and wings of this red-tailed hawk identify it as a buteo.

The shape of a hawk's wings and tail tells a lot about where the bird lives. Hawks that hunt mostly in open country such as prairies, arctic tundra, meadows, fields, and marshes usually have long, wide wings and a short, broad tail. Their large wings and tail help them to circle and soar higher and higher into the sky without having to flap and do much work. Twelve of the 16 species (SPEE-sees), or kinds, of hawks that live in the United States and Canada are built like this. Scientists call them buteos (BEWT-ee-ohs), or soaring hawks.

The northern goshawk fans its long tail to slow its speed before it lands.

Three other species of hawks live and hunt in thick forests where there are tree trunks and branches that can interfere with flying. These hawks, which scientists call accipiters (ack-SIP-ih-turs), have short, rounded wings and a long tail. When they fly, they usually do not soar. Instead, they flap and glide through the trees. Their short wings allow them to pick up speed quickly, and their long tail helps them to swerve and change directions rapidly, something the soaring hawks cannot do.

Only the northern harrier has bright white rump feathers, which is an easy way to identify this hawk.

One other hawk, the northern harrier, has a different shape from all the rest and belongs in a group by itself. Harriers have long, narrow wings and a long tail. The long wings and tail help it to fly slowly and quietly, close to the ground, so it can listen for prey. It frequently hunts in meadows and marshes, where there are no trees to avoid, so it does not need the ability to dodge and swerve quickly like an accipiter.

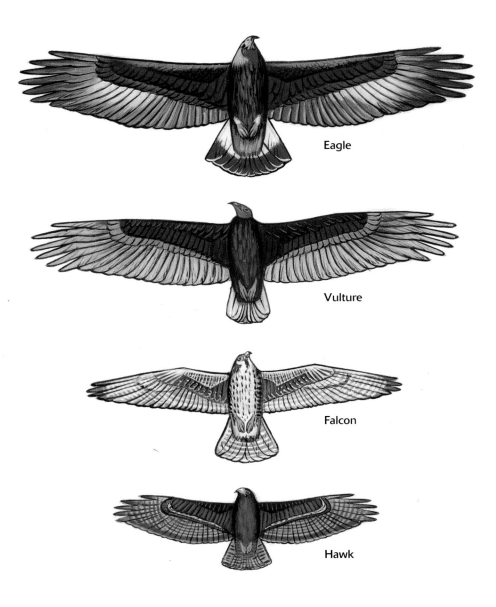

Eagle

Vulture

Falcon

Hawk

The shape of a raptor's wings and tail differ
depending upon whether it soars, flaps, or dives.

17

A bold male red-winged blackbird chases away a female northern harrier that flew too close to its nest.

Hawks, like most birds of prey, are meat eaters, but what they eat depends on where they live. Rough-legged hawks in the Arctic mostly eat small rodents called lemmings. Red-tailed hawks in central Washington munch on different kinds of snakes, while red-tails in Utah hunt jackrabbits. Red-shouldered hawks in Michigan eat crayfish, frogs, and toads. Cooper's hawks in the prairies chase robins, doves, and sparrows. Throughout most of the prairies, Swainson's hawks eat ground squirrels, but on the Oklahoma prairies some of these hawks hunt bats as they pour out of their caves at nightfall to search for insects.

Hawks hunt in different ways. The soaring hawks, or buteos, often hunt while flying. They circle high in the sky, watching for a careless animal that might become their next meal. When they spot a target, they quickly drop out of the sky and swoop in for the kill. If they can, they hide their final approach by flying behind a hill or some trees or shrubs. Then they attack by surprise. Even though the soaring hawks are masters of flight, they hunt more often by standing still. First they find an elevated perch such as a tree branch, a telephone pole, or the edge of a cliff. Then they stand and stare. When something flutters, runs, or wiggles, the sharp-eyed hawk dives with a foot full of talons.

Hawks
FUNFACT:

Small songbirds, crows, and jays will often mob a hawk that is perched nearby to drive it away. The birds swoop around the hawk in groups and call noisily to attract attention. Red-winged blackbirds and kingbirds are bold enough to actually attack a hawk and peck it.

The northern goshawk commonly hunts ruffed grouse, especially male grouse, which are less careful during the spring breeding season.

The forest-hunting accipiters are sneaky hunters. Often they hide among the branches of a tree. Then when a songbird passes nearby, they explode from their hiding place with lightning speed, and grab the victim in a puff of feathers. If the songbird swerves and flees, the chase is on. The hunter and the hunted zigzag through the forest in a race almost too fast to follow. Most times, the songbird wins the race and the hungry hawk goes back to hide and sneak again.

When a red-tailed hawk makes a kill, it often moves the prey to an elevated perch where it is safer to eat.

Harriers and some buteos, especially the rough-legged hawk, hunt by flying slowly, back and forth, close to the ground. Mice and voles can only see things close up, so hawks that hunt like this are invisible to their prey. When the searching hawk hears a squeak or sees the grass move, it may hover for a moment to pinpoint the target. Then, with its feet outstretched, it drops like a rock and snatches the mouse. Often, though, the hawk misses and the mouse lives to squeak another day.

White-tailed hawks commonly hunt animals as they flee from the flames of prairie grass fires.

Even though hawks are skillful hunters, they often go hungry. They must use every trick they know to catch a meal. Two southern hawks have an unusual way of catching prey. In Texas, the white-tailed hawks watch for prairie fires, and as many as 60 hawks may fly in for dinner. The fire-loving hawks hover in the choking smoke or drift back and forth in front of the flames, gobbling up lizards, snakes, insects, and rodents fleeing for their lives. Behind the flames, other hawks search the burned grasses for critters that did not survive.

Texas and Arizona are home to another hawk with a surprising way to hunt. The Harris's hawk of the desert hunts in packs, something that no other hawk in the world is known to do. Packs of five hawks are the most common, and the birds are always related to each other. Usually one or both parents and their young join together. Their favorite prey are desert cottontails, ground squirrels, and wood rats. The birds chase their prey in relay races to tire it out, or they surprise it by attacking from different directions at once. Another trick is for one or two birds to chase the prey on foot and flush it into the open, where it is attacked by another hawk that was perched and waiting.

Hawks
FUNFACT:

The most common hawk in North America is the red-tailed hawk. It lives everywhere from the arctic tree line to Mexico.

Three fledgling Harris's hawks perch on a cactus, waiting for their parents to feed them. A fledgling is a young bird that has left the nest.

Some hawk prey fight back. Many red-tailed hawks have scars on their legs from sharp-toothed mammals such as rabbits, hares, and squirrels. One scientist saw a red-tailed hawk attack a weasel and try to fly away with it, but the angry weasel bit and killed the hawk in self defense.

Another animal that may fight back is a rattlesnake, and rattlesnake venom can kill a hawk. Even so, different hawks try their luck with the deadly snakes, and the hawk usually wins. The snake strikes the bird in the body or wings and gets nothing but a mouth full of feathers. The hawk then kills the snake by pecking it on the head.

One kind of animal that never fights back is a dead one. Hawks that live on the prairies and in the Arctic seem especially good at finding dead animals, called carrion (CARE-ee-un). It may be the lack of trees that makes the carcasses (KAR-kus-iz), or dead bodies, easier to locate. Red-tailed hawks, Swainson's hawks, rough-legged hawks, and northern harriers all eat carrion.

Winter can be one of the biggest killers of wildlife, and many hawks eat carrion in early spring when live prey may be scarce, or hard to find. Another wildlife killer is the automobile, and many hawks eat the flattened carcasses on the roadways. Sometimes these feasting hawks stuff themselves so full they cannot fly away quickly enough and are killed by other vehicles that drive by.

If a hawk cannot catch its own food, or find some that is already dead, it can always become a pirate and steal from others. This is common among hawks. The red-tailed hawk is large and powerful, and it steals meals from rough-legged hawks, northern harriers, peregrine (PER-uh-gren) falcons, and prairie falcons. The harriers and short-eared owls often steal from each other.

A snow goose is too large for a harrier to kill.
This goose was already dead when the harrier found it.

Adult Swainson's hawks scream loudly whenever a predator approaches their nest.

Hawks may use calls to try to scare away others stealing their food or invading their territory. They use their calls for many other reasons, too. Hawks call to search for a mate, or they yell to brag that they own a piece of prairie or patch of forest and that they will defend it from outsiders.

Different hawks have different calls. Some scream and whistle, and others squeak or bark, sometimes from a perch, sometimes from the ground, and sometimes from high in the sky. The steam-whistle scream of the red-tailed hawk is the most familiar call of any hawk in North America, because the cry of this hawk has been used in many movies and on television.

Hawks are noisiest during the spring when it is time to raise a family.

When hawks are ready to mate, the first thing they do is to scream to let others know. Partners often call together, circle and soar together, and sky dance. In sky dancing, the male, and sometimes the female, swoops up and down across the sky in the pattern of a giant roller coaster. Other times, the male flies above his partner and then dives toward her. Just before they collide, the female flips upside down and the two birds briefly touch talons, like friends holding hands.

Many hawks have the same partner for several years, and some may mate for life. Others, such as the northern harrier, have a different partner every spring. Some male harriers may have seven female partners during a single mating season!

The red-shouldered hawk lives in woodlands where its call may be heard even though the bird may stay hidden.

The parents of these Swainson's hawk eggs used fresh aspen twigs and leaves to build their nest.

All hawks build nests. The most common place is in a tree. In places where there are no trees, the birds nest on cliffs or on the ground. A pair of hawks may repair an old nest from a past season or build a new one. Usually, both the male and the female gather twigs, bark, and grass for the nest, but the female does all the building.

A hundred and fifty years ago on the prairies, ferruginous (feh-ROO-juh-nus) hawks sometimes built nests using old bison ribs and lined the nest with the wool from these shaggy beasts. Today, with many bison gone, the hawks use sticks and chips of dried cattle dung.

One of the most interesting habits of nesting hawks is their use of green leaves and twigs in building their nests. Often, they start doing this before they even lay eggs. Many pairs continue to add fresh greenery until the chicks are quite large. The most likely reason they do this is to prevent flies, ticks, and fleas from settling in the nest. These pests feed on bird blood and that is harmful to small, helpless chicks. Green plants such as pine needles and the leaves and twigs of cottonwood trees help to protect the chicks because they produce strong smelling chemicals that insects do not like.

Hawks
FUNFACT:

**Hawk droppings would quickly dirty their nests
if they were not careful. From an early age,
chicks always point their bottoms over the edge
of the nest when they poop.**

Most hawks lay just two to four eggs each year. That is not many when you consider that a gray partridge lays 15 eggs, and a domestic chicken may lay over 300 in a year. Once a female hawk starts to lay her eggs, the male hawk does all the hunting for himself and his partner. In fact, the male hawk may start feeding his mate several weeks before she begins laying. He continues to feed her like a princess for the whole month while she sits on her eggs and warms them. This period is called incubation (ink-you-BAY-shun). Even after the chicks hatch, the male hawk hunts for his entire family until the young are about half grown. A male harrier may catch 40 voles a day to feed his family. One scientist observed a male broad-winged hawk that brought 11 voles, 8 snakes, 5 frogs, and 3 birds to his nest in just three days, and there was only one chick to feed.

Growing chicks have big appetites. After a few weeks, the male hawk cannot hunt fast enough to keep his partner and his chicks filled with food, so the female hawk must start to hunt for the family as well.

Hawks
FUNFACT:

Large hawks live longer than small ones. The red-tailed hawk and ferruginous hawk may live 15 to 20 years, whereas the small sharp-shinned and Cooper's hawks rarely live more than 4 or 5 years.

A female sharp-shinned hawk will brood her chicks, or sit on them to keep them warm, for about 10 days.

This rough-legged hawk chick used the white egg tooth on the tip of its beak to free itself from the eggshell.

Usually a hawk's eggs do not hatch at the same time. As a result, the chicks are different ages and sizes. Naturally, the largest chicks are able to beg the loudest and so are fed first, while the smaller ones get shoved out of the way. When there is a lot of food this is not a problem. The smaller chicks simply wait until their larger nest mates are full, and then they can eat. When prey is scarce, however, it is a different story. The largest chicks hog all the food, and the smaller chicks go hungry and may even starve. In Swainson's hawks and rough-legged hawks, the largest chicks may even attack their smaller brothers and sisters and peck them to death. The parents never try to stop these deadly food fights.

When a chick starves or is killed, it also may be eaten. The mother hawk may tear it up and feed it to her other

This female northern harrier feeds her chick small bits of meat until it is strong enough to feed itself.

chicks or she may eat it herself. When food is scarce, nothing is wasted.

Although the adult male hawk does the hunting for the family, only the female feeds the chicks. Usually when a male returns with food he screams to his mate. He may stop at a special perch nearby, called a plucking post. The plucking post is usually an old nest, a log on the forest floor, or a large limb on a tree. Here the male prepares the prey for his family. If the meal is a songbird or small mammal, he usually cuts off the head and eats that himself. Then he plucks out some of the feathers or fur and removes and eats the insides. Dinner is now ready to be served. The female hawk flies over and collects the meal, or the male delivers it directly to her at the nest. The male hawk never stays around for dinner, and the female always feeds the chicks alone.

Young Cooper's hawks spend a month in the nest after which they hop to branches nearby.

At first, when the chicks are still balls of white fuzz, they are fed tiny bits of meat. As they get older, the bits get bigger. By the time they are three or four weeks old the chicks can feed themselves. The hungry chicks squabble and steal from each other. They guard their meals by spreading their wings over the food to hide it from the others. This guarding behavior, called mantling (MANT-ling), is something a young hawk will do for the rest of its life whenever it catches a meal and wants to hide it from other hawks.

At this stage in the nesting cycle, the parents will fiercely defend their young and often attack animals that might be a threat. They have spent several months of hard work raising their family and they want the chicks to survive. If a predator (PRED-uh-tor), such as a great horned owl or coyote, comes near the nest, the adults may attack. They may also attack other hawks, eagles, or wildlife photographers that get too close. A ferruginous hawk will attack a red fox half a mile from its nest and strike the animal so hard that it knocks it over. The taloned feet of an angry northern goshawk can strike at 50 miles per hour (80 kph). Such a blow can seriously injure even an animal as big as a black bear that is foolish enough to climb up to the bird's nest. Few bears are so brave or so hungry.

Hawks
FUNFACT:

Hawks are not brightly colored. Most are brown, black, or gray on top and pale with streaks underneath.

The prairie Swainson's hawk is especially fierce in defending its nest and young. The male patrols from high in the sky and dives on any trespassers. They try to rake their enemies with their sharp talons to drive them away. Even crows and harmless turkey vultures (VULL-churz) may be attacked. If the trespasser is another Swainson's hawk the two birds may lock talons in a midair battle, and spiral, or twist, through the air. Most of the time, the fighters separate and neither is injured. Sometimes, however, the hawks get badly cut, break a wing, or even die if they crash into the ground.

Hawks
FUNFACT:

At the base of every hawk's beak is a bright yellow fleshy area called the cere (SEAR). There are no feathers on the cere and this may help the hawk keep its face clean and free of blood when it feeds on fresh prey.

The necks on these young Swainson's hawk chicks are swollen because they have just been fed by their mother.

Snakes, including venomous rattlesnakes, are a common food in the diet of the red-tailed hawk.

At four to six weeks of age, most hawk chicks are ready to leave home. They usually cannot fly well yet, but they can flutter, hop, and jump, and that is what they do. They jump out of the nest and hop along nearby branches. Scientists call these young hawks "branchers." For the next month or two, the hawk parents will continue to feed their chicks as they become stronger and better flyers. At first, the chicks will return to the nest during the day to be fed, and at night to sleep. Eventually, though, the whole family moves away from the nest and none return.

A young fledgling ferruginous hawk on the ground will
defend itself with its strong feet and sharp talons.

Adult hawks do not teach their chicks to hunt. The chicks must learn on their own. At first, the young hawks will chase each other, attack sticks and clumps of mud, and practice diving and landing. Many young hawks will jump about in the grass to catch crickets, grasshoppers, lizards, and small snakes. Some will steal food from their nest mates, their parents, or other adults. Carrion may also be important to young hawks still learning to hunt.

The most difficult time in a young hawk's life is the first weeks and months after its parents stop the free meals. This is when they must hunt or starve. In good years, only half the young hawks die. In bad years, most will die before they are one year old. A lack of food kills most of them, but some die in crashes with automobiles or power lines. Others are killed by larger hawks or by great horned owls, one of the most powerful raptors in North America.

A northern goshawk mantles over a freshly killed ruffed grouse. This behavior hides the dead bird from thieves such as ravens and other goshawks.

The Harris's hawk, which lives in deserts, does not need to migrate in winter and lives in its territory year-round.

When deep snow covers the ground, it is difficult for a hawk to find food. Because of this, most of the hawks that live in the arctic tundra and the northern forests of Canada and Alaska migrate in winter. Most fly south to the United States and Mexico where the winters are warmer. Some, such as the broad-winged hawk and Swainson's hawk, are long-distance travelers and journey all the way to South America. Both soar in great flocks for several months to reach their wintering grounds.

In the autumn, a bird-watcher may see a thousand of these hawks soaring overhead in a single day as they fly south, an event that thrills more and more people every year. Hawk watching was not always such a popular pastime. Just a hundred years ago, hawks were poisoned and shot as pests. Rewards were paid for their severed, or cut off, feet. People thought hawks were mean, bloodthirsty beasts, and that the only good hawk was a dead hawk. Today, people think differently. All hawks are protected. They are an important part of a healthy wild world and they need protection so that future children can enjoy these magnificent birds of prey.

Internet Sites

You can find out more interesting information about hawks and lots of other wildlife by visiting these Internet sites.

www.adoptabird.org/	Adopt-A-Bird
http://museum.gov.ns.ca/mnh/nature/nsbirds/bns0087.htm	Birds of Nova Scotia
www.buteo.com/idhelp.html	Birds of Prey at Buteo.com
www.desertusa.com/aug96/du_hawk.html	Desert USA
www.enchantedlearning.com	Enchanted Learning.com
www.ggro.org/idhelp.html	Golden Gate Raptor Observatory
www.pbs.org/wnet/nature/exbirds/warriors.html	PBS Online
www.peregrinefund.org/Explore_Raptors/index.html	Peregrine Fund
www.raptor.cvm.umn.edu/	The Raptor Center at the University of Minnesota
www.worldalmanacforkids.com/explore/animals/hawk.html	World Almanac for Kids Online

Index

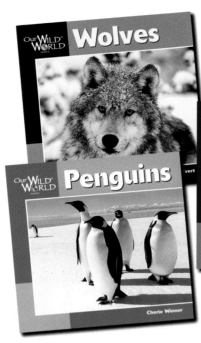

ALLIGATORS AND CROCODILES ISBN 1-55971-859-5	**LEOPARDS** ISBN 1-55971-796-3	**SEA TURTLES** ISBN 1-55971-746-7
BISON ISBN 1-55971-775-0	**LIONS** ISBN 1-55971-787-4	**SEALS** ISBN 1-55971-826-9
BLACK BEARS ISBN 1-55971-742-4	**LIZARDS** ISBN 1-55971-857-9	**SHARKS** ISBN 1-55971-779-3
CARIBOU ISBN 1-55971-812-9	**MANATEES** ISBN 1-55971-778-5	**SNAKES** ISBN 1-55971-855-2
CHIMPANZEES ISBN 1-55971-845-5	**MONKEYS** ISBN 1-55971-849-8	**TIGERS** ISBN 1-55971-797-1
COUGARS ISBN 1-55971-788-2	**MOOSE** ISBN 1-55971-744-0	**TURTLES** ISBN 1-55971-861-7
DOLPHINS ISBN 1-55971-776-9	**ORANGUTANS** ISBN 1-55971-847-1	**WHALES** ISBN 1-55971-780-7
EAGLES ISBN 1-55971-777-7	**PENGUINS** ISBN 1-55971-810-2	**WHITETAIL DEER** ISBN 1-55971-743-2
GORILLAS ISBN 1-55971-843-9	**POLAR BEARS** ISBN 1-55971-828-5	**WILD HORSES** ISBN 1-55971-882-X
HAWKS ISBN 1-55971-886-2	**PRAIRIE DOGS** ISBN 1-55971-884-6	**WOLVES** ISBN 1-55971-748-3

See your nearest bookseller, or order by phone 1-800-328-3895

NorthWord PRESS
Chanhassen, Minnesota